Learn How to Play the Irish Way

ASAP

Irish
GUITAR

by Doc Rossi

ISBN 978-1-57424-288-1
SAN 683-8022

Cover by James Creative Group

CENTERSTREAM®

Copyright © 2012 CENTERSTREAM Publishing, LLC
P.O. Box 17878 - Anaheim Hills, CA 92817

www.centerstream-usa.com

Doc Rossi

CONTENTS

BASIC TECHNIQUE & ORNAMENTATION

The guitar has appeared in recorded examples of Irish traditional music since the early 20th century, and for the past 50 years or so it has become quite common at sessions, on record and in concert. There are a lot of great guitarists playing traditional music now, using a variety of tunings from standard to Drop-D, DADGAD and several others, including one I invented myself. Since the purpose of this book is to give you a quick guide to flatpicking Irish traditional music on the guitar as soon as possible, all of the tunes can be played in standard tuning without a capo. Accompaniments can also be played in standard tuning, but you might prefer to try Drop-D for its extra resonance, bottom end and chord voicings that blend well with this drone-based and often modal music. I've provided diagrams for the voicings I use on the CD.

Ornamentation in traditional music is improvised and spontaneous. I've provided two versions of the first two tunes to give you a basic idea of how ornaments work in context. In the rest of the book, some ornaments and variations are written out where appropriate, giving you a little more insight into which ornaments might be played where. These arrangements are not written in stone: they simply illustrate different ways of gracing notes based on what I've learned from the musicians who taught me.

Most ornaments on the guitar are played using hammer-ons and pull-offs, with the occasional bend or slide. Ornaments should be played quickly, without putting the other notes in the bar out of time. In other words, they "borrow" time from the notes near them. They are really just a flick of a left-hand finger or two and should add bounce and lightness to the tune. The exception to this is the plucked triplet, which is primarily a right-hand ornament. It too should also be played light and bouncy, and often has a more percussive or rhythmic rather than melodic effect.

The tablature follows normal conventions: the top line represents the top or highest-pitched string; the lower represents the sixth or lowest string; numbers represent frets, with 0 being an open string. The rhythm markings are the same as those used in standard guitar notation, meaning that it is slightly simplified to make it easier to read, so you should let some notes ring on longer than indicated. A tie or slur between notes of different pitch indicates that the first note is sounded with the pick, with the note or notes following being hammer-ons, pull-offs or slides. Two parallel slashes in the final measure of some tunes means that the tune ends on the note just before them. Grace notes are smaller than main notes and can be left out when you are first learning a tune.

I use a rather stiff yet thin flatpick, and play with the rounded edge rather than the point. I find this gives me a fuller tone and that the pick glides over the strings more easily. I adjust my grip to make the flatpick more or less flexible as needed. I try to keep my right wrist as loose as possible and in general use an up-and-down motion, except when playing jigs, which are discussed below. My right-hand fingers very lightly touch the top and I often rest my wrist or forearm on the bridge, especially when playing rhythm.

There are some longish stretches for the left hand, and it has to be ready to move up and down the neck to play some passages more smoothly. Other fingerings are possible, but I've decided on these for their simplicity and clarity so that tunes can be played up to tempo pretty quickly.

A single grace note or *acciaccatura* is written as a small eighth note with a line through its stem. They are often placed between notes of the same pitch, or before an important note to give it more emphasis. Pick the grace and pull-off for the main note. [CD track 1]

Double grace notes or trills are written as two sixteenth notes. Pick the first note, then quickly hammer-on and pull-off the next two. [CD track 2]

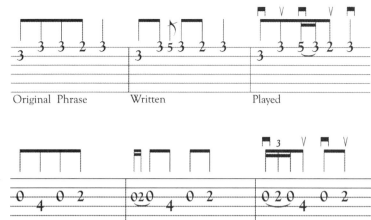

Triplets are three notes played in the place of two. There are several kinds - plucked, slurred, ascending and descending. They are often shown in tune books, but are also used to decorate quarter notes or to fill-in between notes that are more than a step apart.

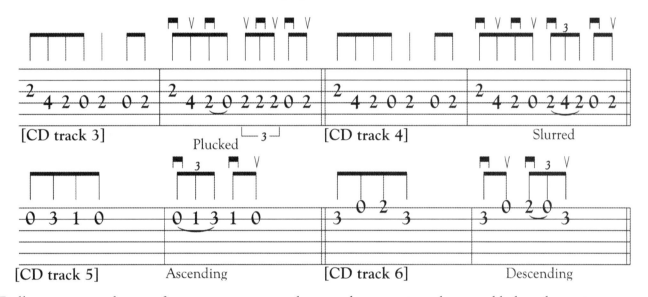

[CD track 3]   Plucked   [CD track 4]   Slurred

[CD track 5]   Ascending   [CD track 6]   Descending

Rolls or turns are four- or five-note ornaments that use the notes just above and below the main note. Often simplified to triplets on plucked instruments, they are used to decorate quarter notes and dotted quarter notes, or a group of quarter and eighth notes of the same pitch.

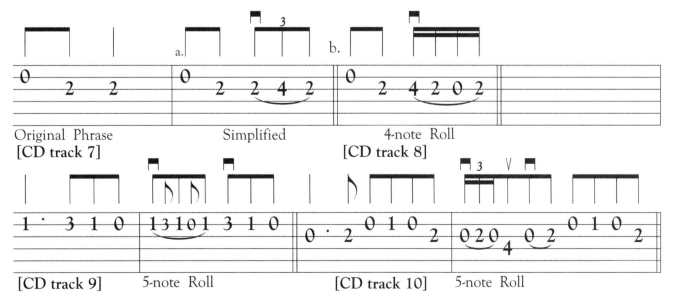

Original Phrase   Simplified   4-note Roll
[CD track 7]   [CD track 8]

[CD track 9]   5-note Roll   [CD track 10]   5-note Roll

Cranning or popping is a technique used by pipers on the low D or E. It is played by lifting off single fingers in quick succession to achieve a bubbling effect. We can imitate this on the guitar by using a quick succession of one hammer-on and two pull-offs.

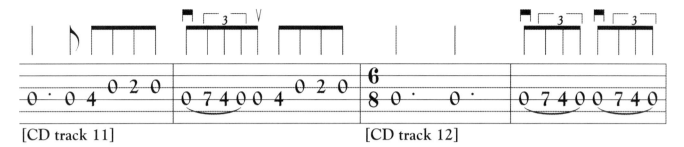

[CD track 11]   [CD track 12]

The guitar has a lot of sustain, so a note ringing on without any added ornamentation can be very effective, as can adding harmony notes or chords. Keep in mind that ornamentation can be overdone. Silence and space are often overlooked elements of tasteful playing.

Although the typical I IV V (ex. D G A) three-chord trick does occur in Irish traditional music, there are other typical patterns to learn as well. Many tunes are in the Mixolydian mode - the major scale with a flat 7th - using chords I IV and VII, for example D G C for the key of D, or A D G for A. Still others combine the major scale (Ionian mode) with the Mixolydian and use four chords, as in **The Floating Crowbar.** Minor tunes have their own three-chord tricks with progressions using Am G F or Em D C. Several tunes, such as **The Banks of Lough Gowna,** switch between minor and major tonalities. Substitutions can be very effective, giving added interest and "lift" to a tune. Typical substitutions are the relative minors - Bm for D, Am for C, Em for G, F#m for A - but there are others, too, like FM7 and Am or CM7 and Em. Because so much of this music is drone based, partial chords and voicings that use suspended 9ths, 6ths or 4ths can also sound effective.

For right-hand patterns, I tend to use the basic eighth-note rhythm of the tune as the basis and vary it from there according to the tune and the players. It can be a lot like playing tuned percussion rather than the typical guitaristic boom-chick. For example, the basic reel rhythm would be 1 & 2 & 3 & 4 &, using alternating down and up strokes. Hornpipes would have a more relaxed feel in 2 rather than 4 and are slower. Jigs are a little different, using a pattern of two groups of three - down up down down up down. These are the basic patterns; listen to the CD for patterns using back beats and other variations.

Here are some useful chord shapes in Drop-D, beginning with D chords.

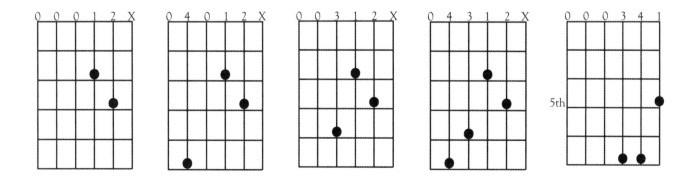

The first two are D chords without thirds, the other three include thirds. The example at the fifth fret is effective when sliding up from the third fret, so moving from C or Am7 to D.

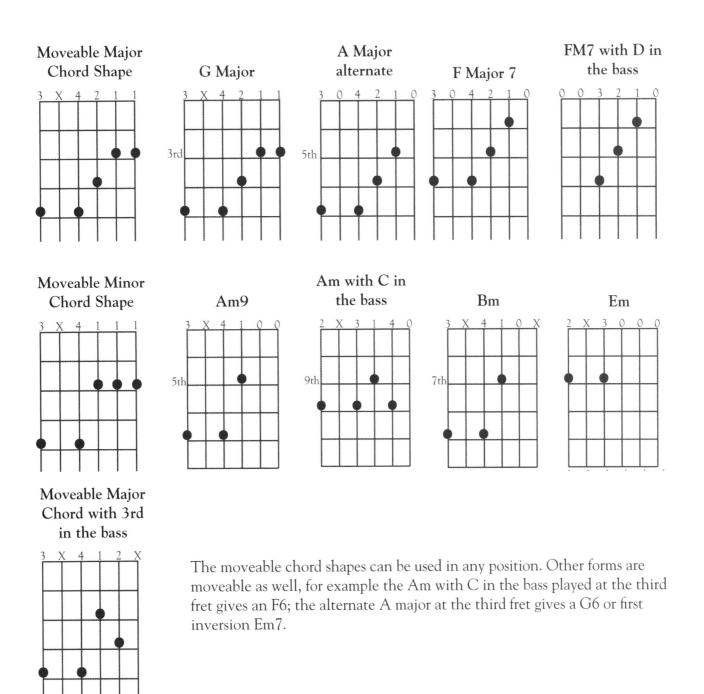

Moveable Major Chord Shape

G Major

A Major alternate

F Major 7

FM7 with D in the bass

Moveable Minor Chord Shape

Am9

Am with C in the bass

Bm

Em

Moveable Major Chord with 3rd in the bass

The moveable chord shapes can be used in any position. Other forms are moveable as well, for example the Am with C in the bass played at the third fret gives an F6; the alternate A major at the third fret gives a G6 or first inversion Em7.

ḣoꞅɴpipes

Hornpipes have an almost funky 2/4 feel. **CD track 13** illustrates the basic accompaniment. **The Fairies Hornpipe** is made up of three strands - measures 1-4, 5-8 and 9-12. Measures 13-16 are the same as 5-8, but note the descending triplet in measure 15 - this is a typical ornament or variation. **The Peacock's Feather** has a similar structure and several descending triplets. The first version of each is the basic tune, the second gives typical ornaments. The ornamented versions follow the basic versions on the CD.

I learned the **Greencastle** and **Liverpool** hornpipes from the great Anglo concertina player Roger Digby. The Greencastle will help you to get familiar with fingerings up the neck. In the Liverpool, the last four measures of each part are the same, so the B part shows variations you can use, while the recording demonstrates others.

The Rights of Man is a popular session tune that will give you more practice with fingerings up the neck. Measures 5 and 6 give an ornamented version of the first two measures.

the peacock's feather ~ basic version

CD tracks 14 & 15

the peacock's feather ~ with ornaments

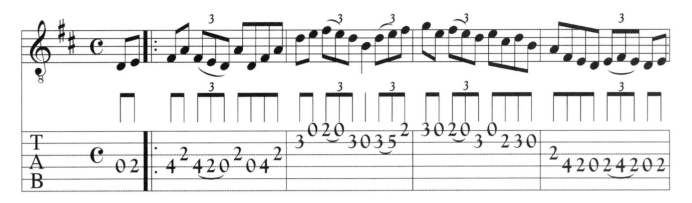

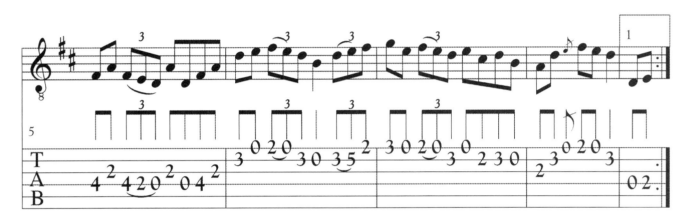

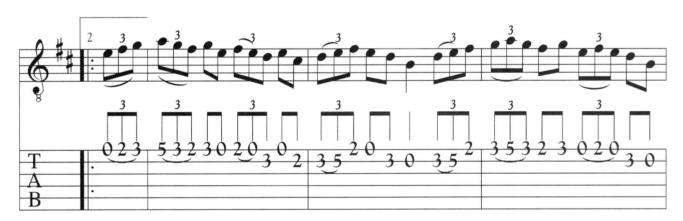

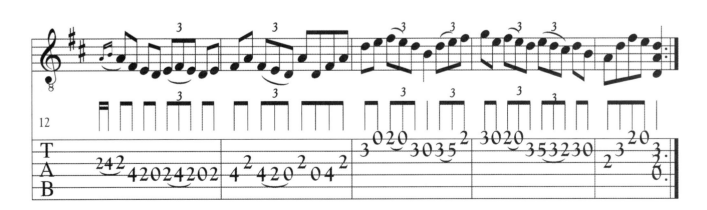

9

the fairies hornpipe ～ basic version

CD tracks 16 & 17

The Fairies Hornpipe ~ With Ornaments

11

the greencastle hornpipe

CD tracks 18 & 19

The Liverpool Hornpipe

CD tracks 20 & 21

13

The Rights of Man

CD tracks 22 & 23

14

JIGS

Jigs are in 6/8 time. They can be counted 123 456, as two groups of three. **CD tracks 24 and 25** illustrate two basic accompaniment patterns. You can also think of jig rhythm as a shuffle - long short / long short. There are different ways to pick jigs; the two most common I've seen traditional banjo players use are down-up-down/down-up-down and down-up-down/up-down-up, with string crossings sometimes breaking the pattern. I favor the first pattern because I like the drive it naturally has, but it does have the awkward feature of consecutive downstrokes, which can sometimes be tricky in quick tunes. In addition to adding more drive and interest, ornaments can also make a tricky passage easier to play by breaking the picking pattern with hammer-ons, pull-offs or plucked triplets, which in jigs look like this:

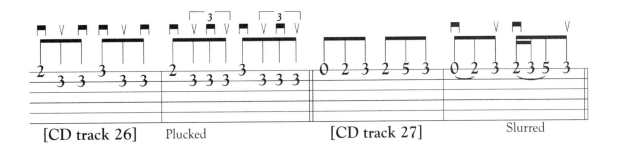

[CD track 26]   Plucked   [CD track 27]   Slurred

Fasten the Leg is a fairly simple classic jig still heard at sessions. Measure five is the same as the first measure, so I've inserted a plucked triplet as a variation. **The Swallow Tail** is a popular session tune in Em. I've left it unornamented, but you should eventually add plucked triplets and other ornaments throughout - listen to the recording.

The Humours of Ballyloughlin is a fine, driving tune that is perfect for learning to master plucked triplets and crans, which have been written out in full.

The Banks of Lough Gowna is in Bm, switching to D in the B part. There are several ways of ornamenting the repeated notes in measures 1 and 5 and the dotted quarters in measures 9 and 13. Note how you jump to the fifth position on the open e in the B part.

The Mist-covered Mountain has an ethereal quality to it, as its title implies. This quality can be enhanced by not playing it too quickly, and by plucking individual notes rather than strumming the accompaniment.

An Phis Fhliuch is a classic slip jig from the piping of Willy Clancy. Slip jigs and hop jigs are in 9/8 time - three beats per measure with the dotted quarter having one beat. **CD track 38** illustrates the basic accompaniment. I learned this tune off one of Willy Clancy's Topic recordings and have tried to adapt some of his ornaments and variations to the guitar. Rather than playing chords, try playing a continuos drone with the basic D chord, adding notes to it rather than full chords. Some suggestions are given below.

Fasten the Leg

CD tracks 28 & 29

The Swallow Tail Jig

CD tracks 30 & 31

humours of ballyloughlin

CD tracks 32 & 33

19

ᴄʜᴇ ʙᴀɴᴋꜱ ᴏꜰ ʟᴏᴜɢʜ ɢᴏᴡɴᴀ

CD tracks 34 & 35

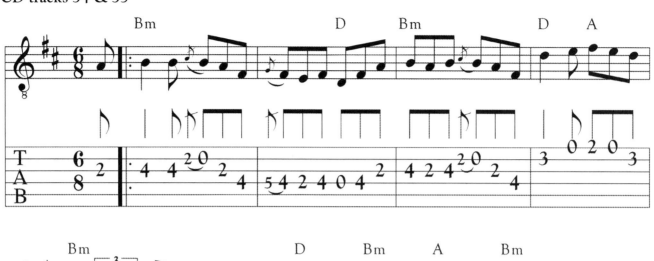

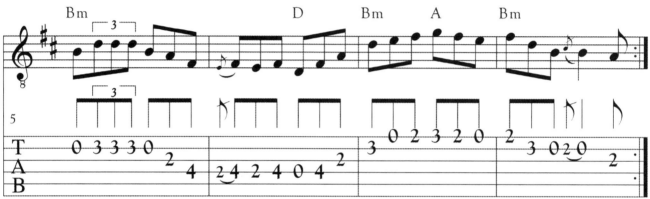

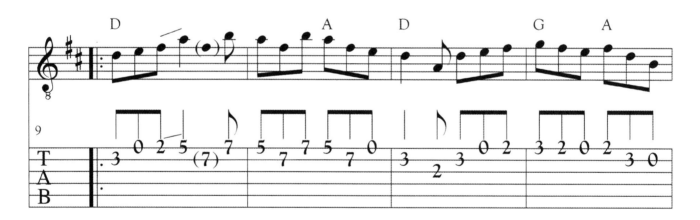

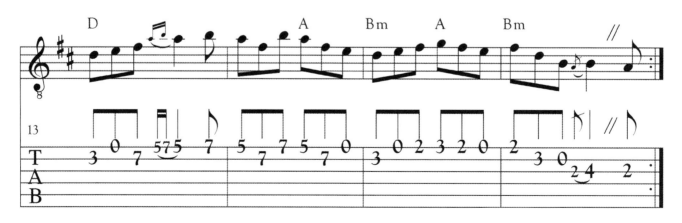

Several traditional tunes have their A parts in a minor key with the B part all or partly in the relative major. **The Banks of Lough Gowna** is such a tune, with the A part in Bm and the B part moving to D. The recording offers three different chord progressions to give you some ideas about how to use chord substitutions. The first time through, the tune is accompanied with the basic chords shown at the left, played in the first position. For the second and third times through, some of the Bm chords are substituted by G chords, giving the tune a slightly different feel. Rather than being a relative Major/minor substitution, this makes use of the Major 7th sound, while adding step-wise progression up or down in the bass (versions two and three respectively).

For the second time through, the Bm chord in measures 7 and 15 is replaced by a G. For the third time through the Bm chord in measures 8 and 16 is replaced by a G. This substitution is quite effective for setting up the change between Bm and D.

In the second and third times through, the D chord in root position in measures 2 and 6 is replaced by the first inversion, with F# in the bass. This gives the feel of F#m, the V chord in B minor, without clashing with the low D in the melody. Similarly, the A chord in measures 10 and 14 can be first inversions, as in the third time through.

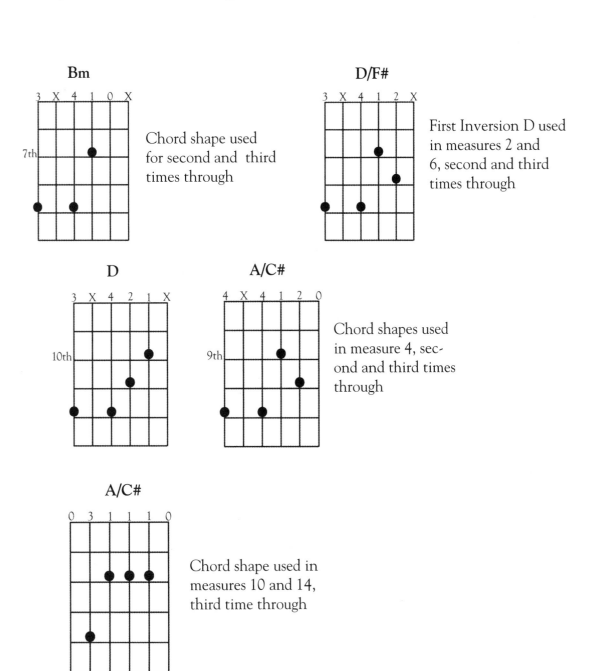

Bm

Chord shape used for second and third times through

D/F#

First Inversion D used in measures 2 and 6, second and third times through

D

A/C#

Chord shapes used in measure 4, second and third times through

A/C#

Chord shape used in measures 10 and 14, third time through

21

the mist-covered mountain

CD tracks 36 & 37

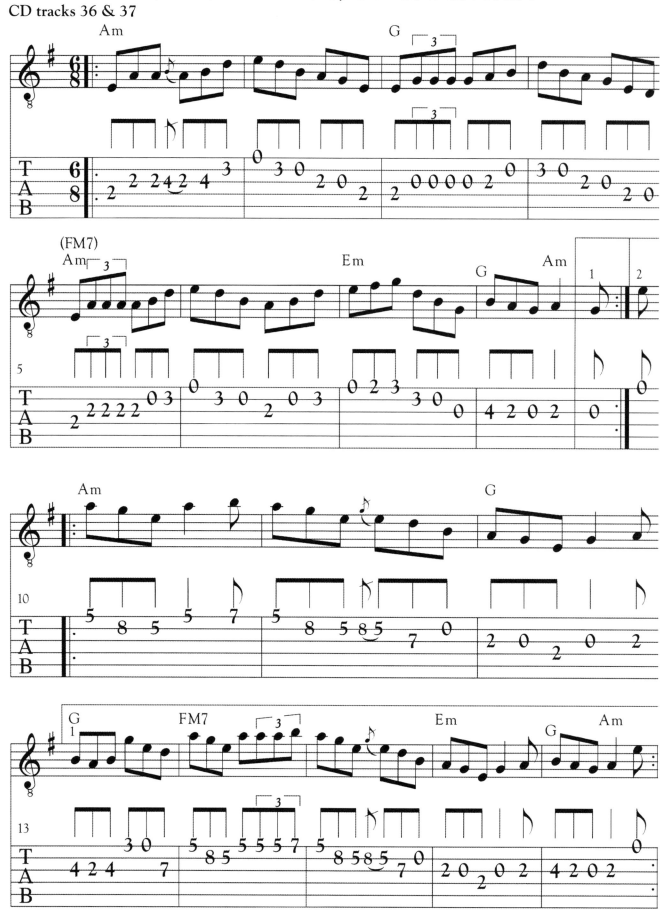

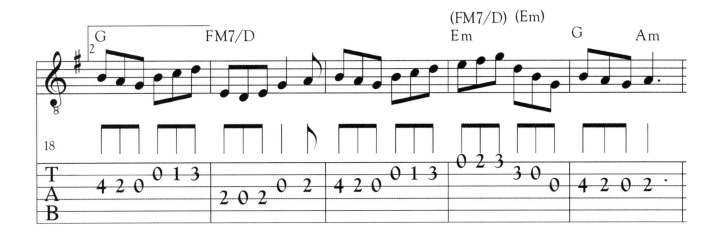

These are some of the chord shapes that I've used on the recording.

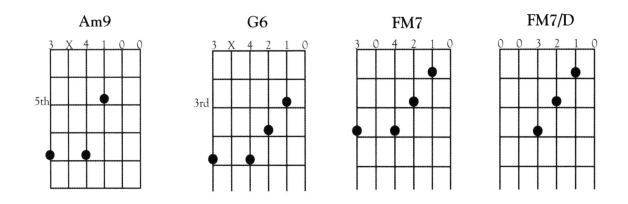

Am9   G6   FM7   FM7/D

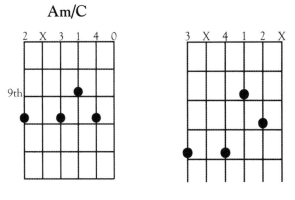

Am/C

This is the moveable first inversion major chord form. When played with the bass note at the 9th fret, it's G with B in the bass; with bass note at the 7th, it's F with A in the bass.

an phis fluch

CD tracks 39 & 40

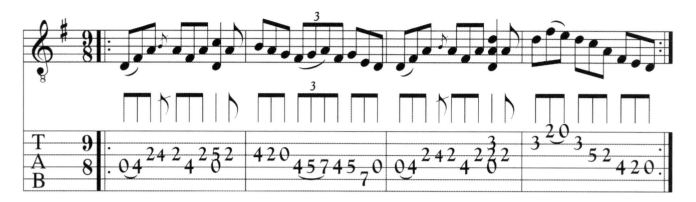

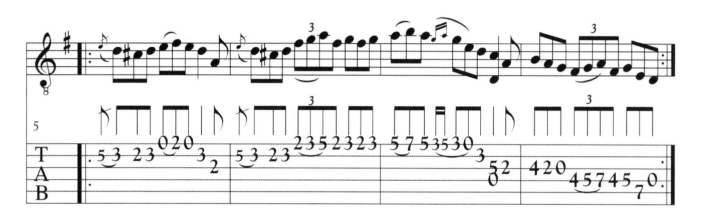

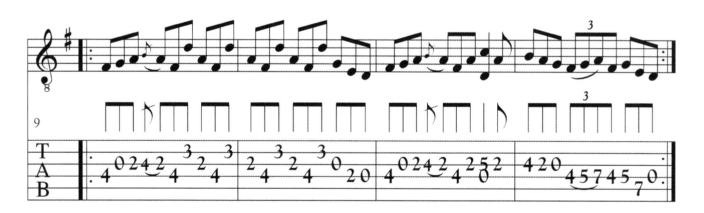

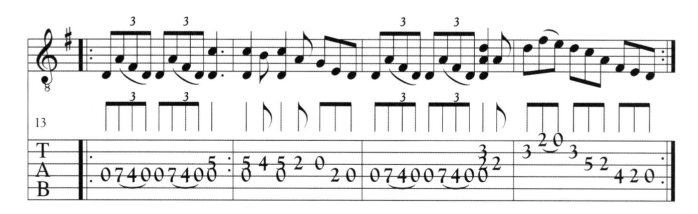

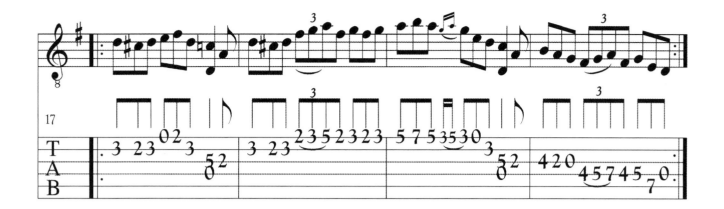

For the recording I drone on the lower strings while holding down the basic D chord, letting the higher strings ring sympathetically. The partial chords shown here can be used at the ends of melodic phrases and cadences to punctuate movement in the tune.

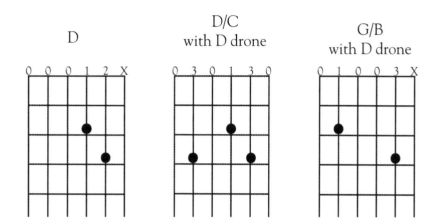

Reels

Reels are straight 4/4, often played quite quickly. The basic accompaniment is illustrated on **CD track 41**.

The Flowers of Michigan is a rare tune with some similarities to the Jug of Punch and **The Temperance Reel**, which flute player Tommy Healy and I used to play together whenever we had the chance.

The Traveller's Reel and **Miss Thorton's** come from The McCusker brothers, a nine-piece ceildh band that recorded a large repertoire of tunes at break-neck speed back in the 1950s. **The Floating Crowbar** is a fine reel that switches between D Mixolydian and D major. Try substituting crans for the triplet figures in measures 1-2 and 5-6.

Rodney's Glory is a set dance that is often played as a hornpipe or a reel. I learned it from Martin Byrnes's excellent Leader LP. He uses a lot of ornamentation in his elegant, lilting style which I've tried to include in this arrangement.

the flowers of michigan

CD tracks 42 & 43

26

The Temperance Reel

CD tracks 44 & 45

The Traveller's Reel

CD tracks 46 & 47

the floating crowbar

CD tracks 48 & 49

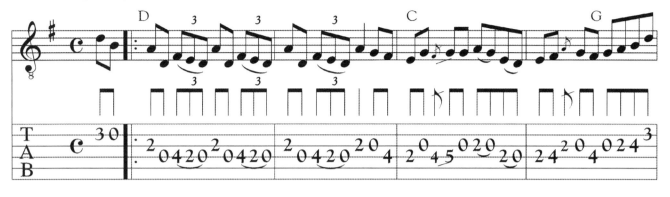

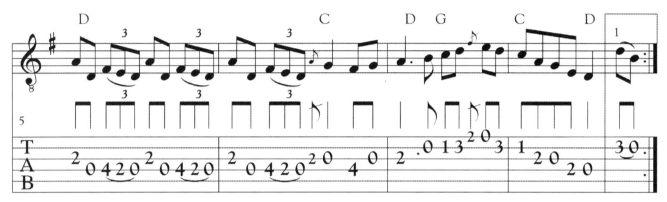

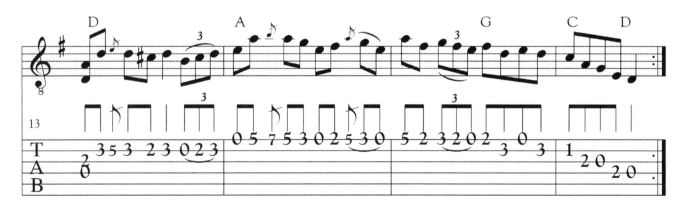

MISS CHORCON'S

CD tracks 50 & 51

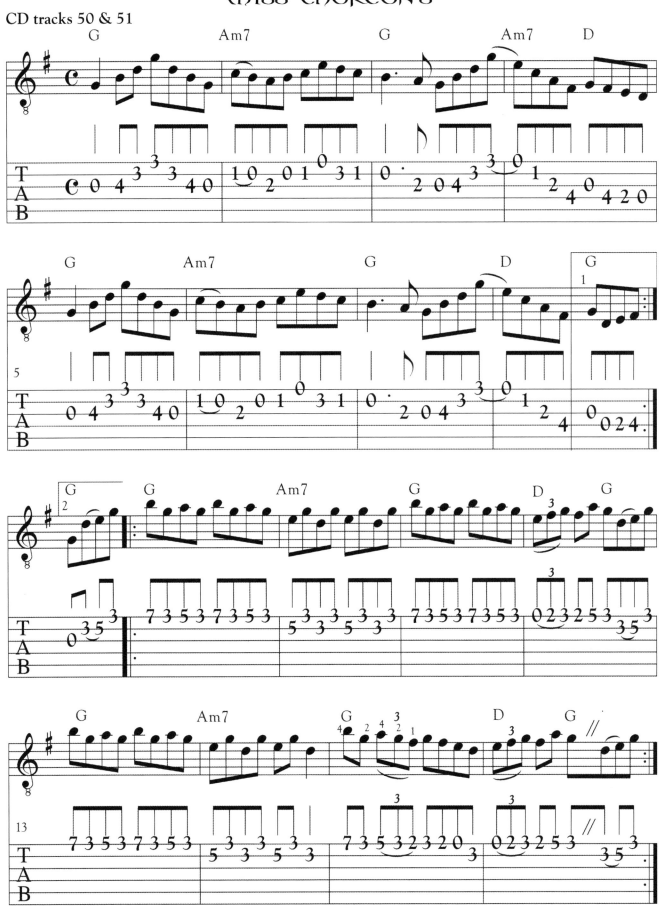

RODNEY'S GLORY

CD Track List

1. Single grace note or *acciaccatura*
2. Double grace notes or trills
3. Plucked Triplet
4. Slurred Triplet
5. Ascending Triplet
6. Descending Triplet
7. Simplified Roll
8. Four-note Roll
9. Five-note Roll, same string
10. Five-note Roll across two strings
11. Cran or Pop 4/4
12. Cran or Pop 6/8
13. Basic Hornpipe Rhythm
14. Peacock's Feather, both versions slow
15. Peacock's Feather, both versions
16. Fairies Hornpipe, both versions slow
17. Fairies Hornpipe, both versions
18. The Greencastle Hornpipe, slow
19. The Greencastle Hornpipe
20. The Liverpool Hornpipe, slow
21. The Liverpool Hornpipe
22. The Rights of Man, slow
23. The Rights of Man
24. Basic Jig Rhythm 1
25. Basic Jig Rhythm 2
26. Plucked Triplet (Jig)
27. Slurred Triplet (Jig)
28. Fasten the Leg, slow
29. Fasten the Leg
30. The Swallow Tail Jig, slow
31. The Swallow Tail Jig
32. The Humours of Ballyloughlin, slow
33. The Humours of Ballyloughlin
34. The Banks of Lough Gowna, slow
35. The Banks of Lough Gowna
36. The Mist-covered Mountain, slow
37. The Mist-covered Mountain
38. Basic Slip Jig Rhythm
39. An Phis Fhliuch, slow
40. An Phis Fhliuch
41. Basic Reel Rhythm
42. The Flowers of Michigan, slow
43. The Flowers of Michigan
44. The Temperance Reel, slow
45. The Temperance Reel
46. The Traveller's Reel, slow
47. The Traveller's Reel
48. The Floating Crowbar, slow
49. The Floating Crowbar
50. Miss Thorton's, slow
51. Miss Thorton's
52. Rodney's Glory, slow
53. Rodney's Glory